OUR · WORLD · MY · ROOTS
GHANA

WRITTEN BY ANNA MAKANDA & SHARMANE BARRETT

ILLUSTRATED BY NATÀLIA JUAN ABELLÓ

OUR DEDICATIONS

In Anna's words:

To my parents, for always believing in me and encouraging me to shoot for the moon. To my mum, for teaching me that in order to know who you are, you must know where you come from. To my husband, for being my absolute rock through thick and thin. To my two beautiful children, who inspire me every day.

In Sharmane's words:

To my parents and my sisters for being my biggest challengers, as well as supporters in life. To my nine amazing nieces and nephews, for being my constant reminder that I need to be a better me for all of the little eyes that are watching.

To all the little explorers,
may you always remember to:

BE CURIOUS

BE CONFIDENT

BE KIND

BE YOU

CONTENTS

NORTH AMERICA

EUROPE

AFRICA

GHANA

SOUTH AMERICA

ANTARCTICA

LOCATION

Ghana is a country in West Africa. It is bordered by the Ivory Coast to the west, Burkina Faso in the north, Togo in the east, and the Gulf of Guinea and the Atlantic Ocean in the South.

Size: 92,099 mi²

Capital: Accra

Currency: Ghanaian Cedi (GHS)

Population: 30 million (2019)

Major Cities: Cape Coast, Kumasi, Tema, Sekondi-Takoradi

Regions: There are 16 regions in Ghana: Ahafo, Ashanti, Bono East, Bono, Central, Eastern, Greater Accra, North East, Northern, Oti, Savannah, Upper East, Upper West, Volta, Western North, Western.

WEATHER

Ghana has a tropical climate where the humidity is high and the temperature ranges between 68 and 86 °F. There are two seasons:

Northern Ghana
Rainy Season: April-October
Dry season: November-March

Southern Ghana
Rainy Season: April-July and September-November
Dry season: August and December-March

LANGUAGES

English is the official language of Ghana. There are 11 additional widely-spoken languages, as well as more than 70 tribal dialects.

RELIGION

Over 70% of the population in Ghana is Christian. The remaining people are Muslim or follow tribal beliefs.

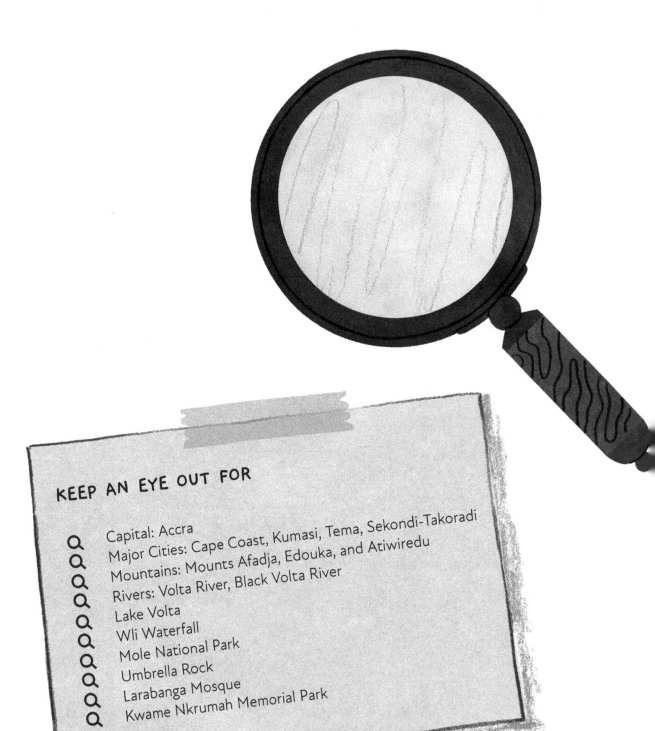

KEEP AN EYE OUT FOR

Capital: Accra
Major Cities: Cape Coast, Kumasi, Tema, Sekondi-Takoradi
Mountains: Mounts Afadja, Edouka, and Atiwiredu
Rivers: Volta River, Black Volta River
Lake Volta
Wli Waterfall
Mole National Park
Umbrella Rock
Larabanga Mosque
Kwame Nkrumah Memorial Park

MOLE
NATIONAL
PARK

LARABANGA
MOSQUE

BLACK VOLTA

EDOUKA

LAKE
VOLTA

AFADJA

WLI
WATERFAL

KUMASI

UMBRELLA
ROCK

ATIWIREDU

VOLTA

ACCRA

SEKONDI-TAKORADI

CAPE
COAST

ARE YOU EXCITED ABOUT GOING ON AN ADVENTURE?

Join us on a journey across land and sea, taking you to Ghana, translated as "Warrior King": the land of gold, diamonds, and cocoa, once known as the gold coast. It is a country with beautiful, rugged scenery, with rolling hills and lush tropical forests, full of an abundance of wildlife. This book will guide you through the country's geography, people, culture, and beyond.

But there's more there than meets the eye. Ghana has a great diversity of languages, communities, beliefs, and traditions. The people of Ghana are known for being very vibrant, respectful, open, and trusting, even when they don't know you. They are strongly rooted in their culture.

You may be surprised to find that even though Ghana is filled with lots of things that are different to where you live, there are many similarities too.

Ghana is more than 41 times smaller than the USA and home to almost 30 million people, who speak approximately 80 different languages.

Perhaps you have Ghanaian heritage and you want to learn more about your roots, or you simply want to learn more about this amazing country. You will find some of the many special things about Ghana in this book, but there is so much more to discover. We hope that you will be able to travel all the way to Ghana and beyond someday.

ENGLISH IS THE OFFICIAL LANGUAGE SPOKEN IN GHANA.

Here is how to say "Hello" in three of the other widely spoken languages:

Some of the other languages include Akuapem Twi, Dagaare, Dagbanli, Dangme Gonja, Hausa, Kasem, and Nzema.

HELLO

AYIKOO
(ASANTE TWI)

MEKYIA WO

(FANTI)

MIAWOE

(EWE)

Throughout the pages of this book you will find many words and phrases translated in:

Asante Twi (red)
Fanti (blue)

HI, WELCOME TO GHANA.

MY NAME IS KOBE AND
I AM 8 YEARS OLD.

THIS IS MY YOUNGER SISTER,
ADWOA. SHE IS 4 YEARS OLD.

AND THIS IS MY BEST FRIEND, KWAME.
HE IS THE SAME AGE AS ME.

WE ARE REALLY EXCITED TO
SHOW YOU AROUND...

LET'S BEGIN OUR ADVENTURE!

MEET MY FAMILY

I live with Adwoa, Mum, Dad, and our grandparents.
We speak Asante Twi and English. I have a big family with lots
of aunts, uncles, and cousins too. Let me introduce you to my...

Family
Ebusuai Abusua

Mum
Maame
Maame

Dad
Papa
Papa

Brother
Nuabanyin
Nuabarima

Sister
Nuabasia
Nuabua

Grandma
Nanabasia
Nanabaa

Grandad
Nanabanyin
Nanabarima

Uncle
Wɔfa
Wɔfa

Auntie
Na
Sewaa

**Cousin
(Female)**
Wɔfa babasia
Sewaa ba

**Cousin
(Male)**
Wɔfa babanyin
Sewaa ba

KWAME'S FAMILY LIVE NEXT DOOR.
They speak Fanti and English.

We call Kwame's mum and dad "Maame" and "Papa" (and any adults my parents' age). We call adults who are our grandparents' age "Ma" and "Wɔfa". This is the respectful way to speak to grown-ups.

DID YOU KNOW?

Ghanaians often have many middle names. There are lots of traditions around naming, including having a name according to the day of the week that we are born on.

Adwoa means "Monday" (she was born on a Monday).
Kobe means "Tuesday".
Kwame means "Saturday".

WHERE WE LIVE

Kwame and I both live in semi-detached houses in Kumasi.

Sewaa Esi lives in a small villa in Takoradi.

My cousins Jojo and Amma live in a bungalow in Cape Coast.

Home
Fie Efie

14

LET'S EXPLORE

LANDSCAPES

Adwoa and I love visiting different parts of Ghana to see the rest of our family. The view on the way is wonderful wherever we go. Sometimes Maame and Papa take the longer route just so we can explore somewhere new. Here are some of the things we have seen along the way...

Explore
Nhwehwɛmu
Hwehwɛ

MOUNTAINS Q

There are ten mountains in Ghana.
These are the three largest:

Mount Afadja, Edouka, Atiwiredu

RIVERS Q

There are 27 rivers in Ghana but there are 2 main ones:

The Volta River is the longest river in Ghana. It starts where the Black Volta and White Volta rivers meet and flows south into the Atlantic Ocean at the Gulf of Guinea.

**Q: How many crocodiles long
is the Volta River?
A: 319,800 crocodiles long—932 mi**

The Black Volta River is smaller than the Volta River. It flows through three countries starting in the highlands of Burkina Faso and ending at Lake Volta reservoir.

**Q: How many crocodiles long
is the Black Volta River?
A: 270,400 crocodiles long—840 mi**

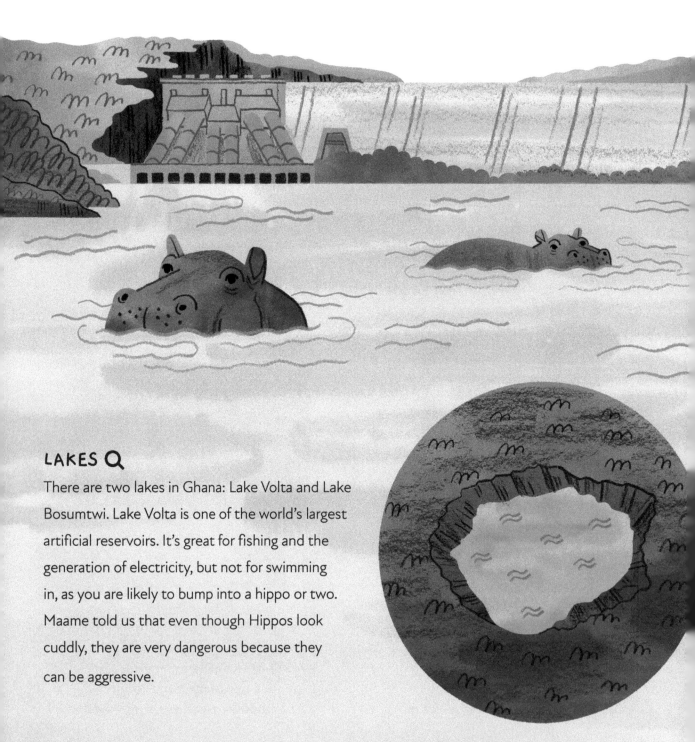

LAKES Q

There are two lakes in Ghana: Lake Volta and Lake Bosumtwi. Lake Volta is one of the world's largest artificial reservoirs. It's great for fishing and the generation of electricity, but not for swimming in, as you are likely to bump into a hippo or two. Maame told us that even though Hippos look cuddly, they are very dangerous because they can be aggressive.

SAVANNAS

These grasslands are flat open spaces with scattered trees, covering two-thirds of the country in the north as well as the coastline in the south. Wild animals such as elephants and lions used to roam the savannas, but now they are mostly found in nature reserves.

DID YOU KNOW?

Ghana is pretty much right at the center of the world; it's both close to the equator and on the Greenwich Meridian (0° longitude).

WATERFALLS Q

There are several waterfalls in Ghana including the Akaa Falls, Agumatsa Falls, and Boti Falls. The largest, most famous waterfall is Wli Waterfall. To find it you need to take a long hike through an ancient forest. The view is beautiful and if you are lucky you can swim in the cold pools at the bottom.

AKAA FALLS

AGUMATSA FALL

BOTI FALLS

FORESTS

Ghana has two types of forest: dry forests in the north, and tropical rainforests in the southwest. The tropical forests are full of evergreen trees, shea trees, acacias, and baobabs.

PLANTS AND TREES

There are thousands of different types of plants and trees in Ghana. Our trees have cool names like bitter kola and African flame tree. Adwoa's favorite is the Adam's apple tree because the name makes her laugh.

Tree
Dua
Dua

DID YOU KNOW?

The toxins in the Impala Lily were once used by the Bushmen as poison for their arrowheads, which they would use when hunting.

FACTS

One of the most important trees in Africa is the shea tree. It can live for 300 years, bear fruit for 200 years, and can grow up to 50ft high and 7ft wide.

The butter from the shea nut is known for its health benefits and various uses. For example people use it for their skin and hair, as well as for medicinal purposes.

The shea tree is a great source of income, especially for women in the northern parts of Ghana who provide for their families. It was known to be used by famous queens, Cleopatra, The Queen of Sheba, and Queen Nefertiti.

THE IMPALA LILY

This is the national flower of Ghana. It can grow up to 7ft high. It is a beautiful flower in the shape of a star, which can be shades of white, pink, and red. It can live all year round. It's also known as a desert rose or Sabi star.

ANIMALS
Mbowa Mmoa

When Boatema and Fosua (our cousins in the US) came
to stay, we went on a trip to Mole National Park. We were all
really excited because we saw lots of antelopes, buffalos, and
elephants—we were even lucky enough to see a leopard. I really
like seeing animals in the wild—they are so magnificent. 🔍

Maame and Papa have promised that next time, we will go to Kakum National Park so that we can walk on the canopy walkway.

HERE ARE SOME OF THE MANY OTHER ANIMALS AND INSECTS YOU MAY FIND IN GHANA—SEE IF YOU CAN SPOT THEM:

Antelope, zebra, African bush elephant, lion, aardvark, hippo, patas monkey, flamingo, honey badger, hyena, pangolin, warthog, wolverine, zebu

DID YOU KNOW?

Baby elephants suck their trunks for comfort.

BOTI FALLS

Last summer, I visited the twin waterfalls at Boti with Kwame and his family. Some people say that the larger of the falls is male and the smaller one is female. During the rainy season, there is a lot of water and the two falls merge. You can see a rainbow in the falling water.

UMBRELLA ROCK 🔍 ~

Umbrella Rock is just a walk away from Boti Falls. It is surrounded by beautiful forests with lots of wildlife. Umbrella Rock got its name because it is a large rock balanced on top of a much smaller rock; it can provide shelter for up to 15 people. It is a good spot to view the mountains and a three-headed palm tree.

CAPE COAST CASTLE

Cape Coast is a city and fishing port in South Ghana. It is one of the most historic cities in the country, and the castle is an important part of Africa's history. It played a significant role in the gold and slave trades.

LARABANGA MOSQUE Q

Built in 1421, Larabanga Mosque is thought to be the oldest mosque in Ghana. The mosque is made of mud and sticks that jut out from the wall (Sudanese-style). It sits right next to a large baobab tree. There is a myth that says the baobab tree has special life-giving powers.

LEGEND HAS IT...

... that the Larabanga stone has "mystical powers". We drove past it on our school trip, on the way to the Larabanga Mosque. Our teacher told us that the builders tried to remove the stone three times when the road was being built, but the next day it reappeared in the same place each time. In the end, they changed the direction of the road.

ACCRA Q

Accra is the most populated city in Ghana. It is also the country's center of business with activities including banking, fishing, and manufacturing.

BLACK STAR GATE

We love to hear Sewaa Esi's stories of attending the Independence Day parades at Black Star Square. She takes a selfie standing under the Independence Arch every time she is there.

KWAME NKRUMAH MEMORIAL PARK & MAUSOLEUM Q

The Kwame Nkrumah Memorial Park is in downtown Accra, and it is dedicated to the prominent Ghanaian President, Kwame Nkrumah. The building represents an upside-down word, which in Akan culture is a symbol of peace. It is covered from top to bottom with marble, and it is surrounded by water, a symbol of life.

LET'S GO TO SCHOOL

SCHOOL

Skuul Sukuu

Kwame and I go to the same elementary school in Kumasi.
We are in the third grade and Adwoa is in kindergarten.

Our school is big with many classrooms. There are lots of fields where
we run around and play sports. We learn in English and also in the Akan
languages. Each day we catch the school bus to and from school.

My cousin, Jojo, goes to school in the rural area of Gomoa District in Cape Coast. Every day, he has to walk a long way to and from school. His school is quite different to ours as it is much smaller, with only a few classrooms.

Homework
Fie dwumadzi
Sukuu mu adwuma
a wcde kc fie kcyj

Student
Adzesuanyi
Cdesuani (Cbaa)

Lesson
Adzesuadze
Adesuadeɛ

Teacher (Female)
Kyerɛkyerɛnyi
Ckyerɛkyerɛni (Cbaa)

Teacher (Male)
Kyerkyerenyi
Ckyerɛkyerɛni (Barima)

WE HAVE THE MOST FUN IN OUR...

MUSIC LESSONS

We play these instruments:

XYLOPHONE

ATENTEBEN
(BAMBOO FLUTE)

AXATSE

AKAN DRUM

SEPEREWA
(HARP-LUTE)

PE LESSONS

At school we play lots of different sports such as soccer, basketball, athletics, table tennis, tennis, and hockey.

DID YOU KNOW?

Like most countries, Ghana's most popular sport is soccer. Their national team is nicknamed the "Black Stars" after the black star of Africa in the Ghanaian flag.

LET'S PLAY

In the playground at school, one
of my favorite games to play is...

AMPE
Players: 4+

Ampe is an active game, with lots of clapping,
singing, and jumping—it almost looks like a
dance. There is one leader and the rest of the
group stand in a semicircle. The leader begins
by jumping and clapping with another player.
Both place one leg forward as they jump. If they
both stick out the same leg, the leader wins a
point. If the legs are different, the next person
becomes the leader. Everyone has a chance to
be the leader and the first person to reach ten
points wins.

Play
Dzi agor
Di agorɔ

LET'S LEARN

NUMBERS

I have been helping Adwoa learn how to count to ten.

Do you want to learn with us?

1 KOR
BAAKO

2 EBIEN
MMIENU

3 EBIASA
MMIENSA

4 ANAN
NNAN

Learn
Sua adze
Sua

5 ENUM
JNUM

6 ESIA
NSIA

7 ESUON
NSON

8 AWƆTWE
NWƆTWE

9 AKRON
NKRON

10 DU
DU

THE ALPHABET

Learning the alphabet is also fun! How many can you say?

A EE
  EE

B BII
  BII

C SII
  SII

D DI
  DI

E I
  I

F ƐF
  JF

G GYII
  GYEE

H EIH
  EIH

I AL
  AI

J GEE
  GEE

K KEE
  KEE

L JL
JL

M ƐM
JM

N ƐN
JN

O O
O

P PI
PI

Q KLW
KIW

R ARR
ARR

S JS
JS

T TII
TII

U UU
UU

V VII
FII

W DEBUU
DCBU U

X ƐKS
JKS

Y WAI
WAI

Z ZƐT
SJT

40

LET'S SAY

Here are some of our everyday words and phrases.
Why not try and say them?

HOW ARE YOU?

W'apɔw mu ɛ?

Wo ho te sɛn?

HOW OLD ARE YOU?

Edzi mfe ahen?

W'adi mfej sjn?

MY NAME IS...

Me dzin dze...

Me din de...

I AM ... YEARS OLD

M'edzi mfe...

M'adi mfej...

GOOD MORNING

Mema wo akye

Maakye

GOOD AFTERNOON

Mema wo aha

Maaha

GOOD NIGHT

Da yie

Da yie

I LOVE YOU

Medɔ wo

Medɔ wo

THANK YOU

Meda wo ase

Medaase

PLEASE

Mepa wo kyɛw

Meserj wo

42

LET'S EAT
FOOD & DRINK

DID YOU KNOW?

The main difference between Ghanaian Jollof and Nigerian Jollof is the type of rice used. Ghanaians use aromatic basmati rice whilst Nigerians use long grain rice, both of which, give a different flavor.

KOBE

I like to eat kooko for breakfast. My favorite dinner is fufu with fried fish, spinach, and okra. It's the most delicious of Maame's dishes.

ADWOA

I like it when Papa cooks breakfast: sweet fried dumplings, plantain, and maasa. Yum yum. My favorite dinner is fante kenkey with gravy stew and chicken.

Yummy
ɔyɛ dɛw
Jyj dj

Eat
Ebedzidzi
Didi

43

KWAME

I like to eat ampesi for breakfast. It's a mixture of cassava, cocoyam, yam, and plantain, boiled with fish and onion. Some days I like to eat eggs with bread—it's nice to mix it up.

My favorite dinner is waakye with meat stew and shito.

There are so many delicious snacks that we all love:

Sugar Bread

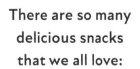

Fried yams with hot chili, lemon juice, and ginger.

Ayigbe biscuits, which are made from tapioca flour.

Nkatie cake, which is made from peanuts.

African fruit—it tastes sweet and sour at the same time.

Shloer, which is a popular drink. Supermalt, which is a soda brewed from barley malt.

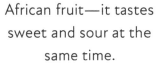

44

PUBLIC HOLIDAYS

We celebrate different public holidays in Ghana. Nanabaa says that we have these days to honor important events and people in history. We have:

7th January: Constitution Day—we celebrate the constitution becoming official in Ghana.

6th March: Independence Day—we honor the heroes of Ghana who led the country to its independence from British colonial rule.

1st May: May Day—a day dedicated to workers around the world.

24th May: Eid ul Fitr—an Islamic festival that marks the end of Ramadan, a month of fasting and prayer.

4th August: Founders' Day—we commemorate the contributions of all the people, especially the "Big Six" who led the struggle for Ghana's independence.

21st September: Kwame Mkrumah Memorial—we remember and honor Ghana's first president, Osagyefo Dr Kwame.

On public holidays, Nanabaa likes the family to get together to celebrate and watch the parades on the TV.

We also celebrate birthdays, Easter, Boxing Day, and New Year's Day. New Year's Eve is a big celebration in Ghana as we want to make sure that we 'cross over' to the next year with as much luck as possible.

LET'S CELEBRATE

We celebrate lots of things in Ghana, from honoring religions and our ancestors (Willa) to rites of passage or the harvest (Gologo festival). Celebrations are different in different parts of Ghana, but they are always grand. We get together with family and friends, get dressed up, eat tasty food, listen to music, and dance all day long. Kwame and his family always have the best parties.

FESTIVALS

In addition to public holidays, there are many festivals celebrated in each village. They are important for all sorts of reasons.

To Celebrate
Yɛngye hɛn enyi
Gye ani

Merry Christmas
Afrenhyia pa
Afe hyia pa

Happy Birthday
Mema wo awoda pa
Mema wo awoda pa

Party
Aponto
Apontɔ

BUGUM

APOO

YAM

ADAE KESE

DIPO

HOMOWO

CHRISTMAS

Festivities begin on 20th December and last until the first week of January. The beginning of Christmas festivities usually happens at the end-of-year cocoa harvest which adds to the feeling of celebration. We play Christmas music on the streets and make ornaments out of crepe paper to take home and hang up in our houses.

On Christmas Day, 25th December, we dress in our traditional clothes and go to church to sing carols and be reminded of the birth of Jesus. We get so excited when Papa Bronya (Father Christmas) comes and leaves us food. We love Christmas!

Sometimes we might get a new pair of shoes or some new clothes. I always eat too much as there is so much tasty food at dinner: jollof rice, chicken stew, curried goat stew, lamb, omo tuo (rice balls), fufu, cassava, and plantain.

GIVING GIFTS

Gift-giving is a big part of our culture. When Maame's friends invite us for dinner, or to a party, she will always take a gift to give to the children. We love it when people come to our house for parties because they bring us gifts too. Our favorites are the pieces that come from Kejetia market. Adwoa loves to collect bracelets.

DRESSING UP

Most of the time, we wear the same kind of clothes that Boatema and Fosua wear in summer in the US. On special occasions, our family gets dressed up in traditional dress, especially for weddings or public holidays like Independence Day. Ghanaian clothes are special because the designs, fabrics, and patterns display our traditional ways of making cloth. It's so fun to wear the bright and colorful kente designs. Every color has a meaning.

EATING

We often eat jollof rice cooked in a stew with chicken for special occasions. The bigger the occasion, the bigger the dinner that is served, like on Christmas Day.

PLAYING MUSIC

Music is a way of life in Ghana; it is important in representing our strong heritage. Traditionally, music was used to affect the atmosphere of a village. People would sing and chant inspirational and motivational songs before an important event. Southern-style music uses drums and gong-gongs, whilst northern-style music uses string instruments and the calabash. Our favorite types of music are Afro pop, Afro jazz, highlife, and hiplife. Sometimes Maame and Papa play traditional music at home or in the car.

DANCING

Dancing cannot be separated from music in our culture, especially drumming. Different drum rhythms mean different things, such as unity, bravery in war, honoring ancestors, and initiation into adulthood. At festivals, the music and dancing is often a social ritual that tells a story or re-enacts an event of historical significance to the tribe. Dances are handed down from generation to generation.

LET'S GET LUCKY

What do you think is lucky or unlucky?
Here are some of ours...

GOOD LUCK

Carrying a "gris-gris"—a small charm
—will keep bad luck away, meaning
good luck will come.

If your right palm itches, it's good
luck and you will come into money.

Dreaming about fish means that
someone you know is going
to have a baby.

If you paint your chickens
fluorescent yellow or pink, they
won't be attacked by baboons.

BAD LUCK

Unless you are the mother, father, or a close relative, you cannot see a newborn baby until the seventh day.

If you pick up money you find on the ground, you will lose more than you found.

It's bad luck to walk around with your hands on your head.

Bathing in warm water will make you age quicker.

Accidentally walking through a cobweb brings bad luck.

LET'S DREAM

Sometimes we close our eyes and dream about what we would like to be when we grow up.

Do you know what you would like to be?

Dream
Ebɔsɔ daa
Daej

MY FAVORITE THING IS TO DRAW PICTURES OF BUILDINGS. WHEN I GROW UP I WANT TO BE AN ARCHITECT LIKE...

SIR DAVID ADJAYE

Sir David Adjaye is an award-winning architect who has designed buildings all over the world. His biggest project is the National Museum of African American History and Culture in Washington DC. Maame told me that he has won many awards for the buildings he has designed.

JUNE SARPONG OBE

My favorite presenter is June Sarpong. I think she's pretty cool. She gets to interview lots of famous people, and she works hard to improve equality.

June is also an author and she now works as the BBC's first Director of Creative Diversity, making sure that all sorts of different people are represented on TV. She does a lot of work for charity. June was awarded an OBE (Officer of the Order of the British Empire) for her services in broadcasting and charity initiatives.

I get good marks at school in my writing classes and so my parents think I would make a great author like...

AFUA HIRSCH

Afua Hirsch was born in Norway to a Ghanaian mother and a British father. She began her career as a lawyer, but she is now an author, TV presenter, and businesswoman. Afua does a lot of work towards creating equality in the world. Maame told me that she is known for being one of the most-influential people of African heritage in the UK.

Adwoa is only four but she loves to dress up in Maame's clothes and look through Maame's magazines. My parents say they can see her being a leader in fashion like...

EDWARD ENNINFUL

Edward Enninful was born in Ghana and moved to the UK as a young boy. He is editor-in-chief of British Vogue magazine, making him its first black editor-in-chief. Edward is not only very influential in the fashion industry but he uses his voice to champion diversity.

Kwame is obsessed with planets. His dream is to build a robot to send into space just like engineer Ashitey Trebi-Ollennu...

ASHITEY TREBI-OLLENNU

Ashitey Trebi-Ollennu was born in Ghana and moved to the UK for university. He is a robotics engineer at NASA, and he became the leader of the team that designed the Mars Rover, the robot that landed on Mars. He founded the Ghana Robotics Academy Foundation, dedicated to motivating and inspiring young Ghanaians in science, technology, and engineering.

WE HOPE THAT YOU HAD FUN EXPLORING GHANA WITH US —KWAME, ADWOA, AND I REALLY ENJOYED SHOWING YOU AROUND. WE HOPE TO SEE YOU BACK SOON!

GOODBYE

NANTE
YIE
(ASANTE TWI)

EKYIR OO
(FANTI)

National anthem

God bless our homeland Ghana
ɔman no ndw
Man no Nnwom

MEANING OF THE FLAG

Red   Represents the blood of those who died in the country's struggle for independence from Great Britain

Gold   Represents the mineral wealth of the country

Green   Symbolizes the country's rich forests and natural wealth

Black star Symbol of African freedom

HISTORY

300-1200	The empire of ancient Ghana ruled, originally under King Dinga Cisse
1471	Portuguese settlers arrived on the coast of Guine
1630-1660	Reign of the Ashanti Empire
1700	Over 100 years of the slave trade began
1807	Trade of cocoa, gold, timber, and palm oil became more popular
1833	Abolition of slavery
1874	Gold Coast became a British colony
1948	Accra riots
1957	Ghana gained independence
1960	Kwame Nkrumah appointed president
1993	Ghana's constitution became official
2007	Ghana celebrated 50 years of independence
2012	Ghana's gold rush (the price of gold rose)

THE AUTHORS

ANNA MAKANDA

Anna was born in Gweru, Zimbabwe, and raised in London, along with her older sister. Her father is Zimbabwean and her mother, Scottish. Growing up, Anna always dreamed of owning her own business. She started her career as an accountant but soon realized it was time to pursue her dreams. That was when she set up her own fitness brand. In her spare time, you will find her spending time with family and friends, chasing after her two very energetic children, or writing a book or two!

SHARMANE BARRETT

Sharmane was born and raised in London, along with her five sisters. Her father is Jamaican and her mother, Trinidadian-English. Growing up, Sharmane was encouraged to pursue a career as a lawyer but after completing her legal studies, she soon realized that law was not for her. She began working in legal recruitment, which gave her an opportunity to live in Singapore for almost four years. Sharmane's passions are travelling and boxing—although these days there is a lot less travelling to exotic destinations, and a lot more time in the gym.

THE ILLUSTRATOR

NATÀLIA JUAN ABELLÓ

Natàlia was born in Barcelona, where she grew up with her older brother, father, and mother. She has loved drawing since she was little and was often found creating and daydreaming as a young girl. Pursuing her dream of working in a creative job, she studied to become a fashion designer but very quickly realized her real passion was to illustrate, especially children's books. Natàlia moved to the UK many years ago and now lives in a small countryside village. She loves nature, and she's happiest when taking long hikes with her partner and little doggy.

OUR GRATITUDE

We would like to say thank you and extend our gratitude to:

Everyone who helped us with the research; Sharmane's wider family, Matilda Addo, our friends Frances Amissah, Beulah Aidoo, and Mitchell Asare, for your advice, opinions, and most importantly, time. Thank you.

Our editor, Amber, who helped us make our facts engaging to our young readers; our copywriter Lisa; our proof-reader, Josie; and Martyn, our wonderful designer, who not only made our books look as beautiful as they do but also helped us articulate our vision so perfectly. To our incredibly talented illustrator, Natàlia, for bringing Kobe, Adwoa and Kwame to life, and for showcasing the magic of Ghana.

And not forgetting all our little people for helping us pick the designs and road-testing the content.

Each other. This is a passion project for us both and to be able to share this journey with a best friend is the dream.

Anna and Sharmane

OUR MISSION

Our mission is to help ignite a child's interest in their roots and empower them to become culturally confident. We aim to do this by providing parents and caregivers factual yet engaging resources to help them teach their children about their culture and heritage.

OUR SOCIAL IMPACT

Children everywhere should have access to education. This is why for every book sold we will be donating a percentage of the proceeds to the OWMR fund which aims to support charities that do exactly that.

COPYRIGHT

A SPECIAL THANKS TO
FAYE-ARIELLE ATTIVOR, AGED 5,
FOR DRAWING THIS
GHANAIAN-INSPIRED PATTERN
(WITH THE HELP OF MUMMY).

Printed in the USA
CPSIA information can be obtained
at www.ICGtesting.com
LVHW070032291023
762437LV00010B/157